20th Century Inventions

CARS

Chris Oxlade

WAYLAND

20th Century Inventions

AIRCRAFT

CARS

COMPUTERS

THE INTERNET

LASERS

MEDICAL ADVANCES

NUCLEAR POWER

ROCKETS AND SPACECRAFT

SATELLITES

TELECOMMUNICATIONS

Cover and title page: The Maclaren F1. Many features of this high-performance car were originally developed for use in racing cars.

Series editor: Philippa Smith
Book editor: Alison Cooper
Series designer: Tim Mayer
Book designer: Malcolm Walker of Kudos Design
Cover designer: Dennis Day

First published in 1997 by Wayland Publishers Limited,
61 Western Road, Hove, East Sussex BN3 1JD, England

Find Wayland on the internet at http://www.wayland.co.uk

British Library Cataloguing in Publication Data
Oxlade, Chris
   Cars. – (Twentieth century inventions)
   1. Automobiles – Juvenile literature
   I. Title II. Benké, Tim
   629.2'22

ISBN 0 7502 2097 X

Picture acknowledgements
Ace 10/Vladimir Pcholkin, 17 (lower)/Rafael Macia, 24/Alexis Sofianopoulos, 35 (top)/P & M Walton, 35 (lower)/Chris King; ActionPlus 28/Peter Tarry; Allsport 26/Matthew Stockman, 27/Mike Hewitt, 29 (lower)/Pascal Rondeau, 31 (lower)/Mike Powell; Neill Bruce 14; Ford Motor Company 17 (top); Ole Steen Hansen 4, 11, 20; Images *cover* (background); Panos 32/Ron Gilings; Popperfoto 39; Quadrant *cover* (main pic) & *title page*, 13/Auto Express, 16 (right)/Auto Express, 18, 22/Autocar, 29/James Lamb, 30/Bryn Williams, 31(top)/Autocar, 43/AutoExpress; Peter Roberts Collection, c/o Neill Bruce 6, 7, 8, 16 (left); Science Photo Library *back cover* & *contents page*/Alfred Pasteka, 37/NASA, 40/Catherine Ponedras/Eurelios, 41/Pater Menzel; Transport Research Laboratory 19; TRH 25/Peter Hogan, 36/E Partridge; Trip 21/C Smedley, 23/ M Beard, 33 (lower)/R Styles; Tony Stone Worldwide 5, 9/Cosmo Condina, 38/Wayne Eastep; Vauxhall Motor Company 41; Wayland Picture Library 33 (top)/Angus Blackburn. Artwork on pages 11, 12, 15, 19, 34 and 42 is by Tim Benké (Top Draw, Tableaux).

Typeset by Malcolm Walker.
Printed and bound in Italy by G. Canale & C.S.p.A., Turin

20th Century Inventions
CONTENTS

CARS EVERYWHERE

Of all the inventions in the history of the world, the motor car has probably made the biggest difference to people's everyday lives, and to the appearance of our towns, cities and countryside. Although the car was invented at the very end of the nineteenth century, all of its impact has been made in the twentieth century. This book looks at the development of the car and at the different types of car (and other vehicles) on the roads today. It also looks at how we use cars and at what driving might be like in the twenty-first century.

Cars give people the freedom to travel where they like, when they like. They take people to school and work. They take them to the shops and carry the shopping home. They can be used to reach places that are difficult to get to in any other way.

Loading the car for a family holiday. Cars have given people a greater choice of ways to spend their leisure time.

Business people use cars to go to meetings or to carry goods. And the whole family can visit friends and relations or travel on holiday in their car.

Cars do cause problems. People waste many hours of their lives sitting in queues of traffic. Exhaust gases from their cars pollute the air and can cause smog in cities. Large areas of the countryside are covered by roads. But the car industry provides work for millions of people, in all sorts of jobs, from making cars to working for oil companies that produce fuel.

Many urban areas are dominated by overhead roads and junctions designed to get traffic in and out of the city quickly.

THE HISTORY OF CARS

The idea of making a self-propelled vehicle was thought of many times in the hundreds of years before the car was invented. The major barrier to building one was finding a way to make the vehicle move. Some inventors had a little success with wind power, but what they really needed was an engine.

Steam power

Soon after the steam engine was invented at the beginning of the eighteenth century, engineers began to build steam-powered vehicles. A steam engine capable of producing enough power to move a vehicle needs to be large and heavy. We say it has a low power-to-weight ratio. In the nineteenth century steam power was used quite successfully in large vehicles, such as trucks and passenger coaches, and, of course, in railway locomotives. But it was impractical for a small and convenient car.

This steam tractor was an early attempt to make a vehicle that moved under its own power. It was built by a French soldier called Nicholas Cugnot in about 1769.

A Benz Sociable, built in 1895, being driven in a vintage car rally. It looks like a horse-drawn carriage without the horse.

A new type of engine

The sort of engine that all modern cars have is an internal combustion engine. 'Internal combustion' means that the fuel burns inside the engine's cylinders, whereas in a steam engine, the fuel makes steam outside the cylinders. An internal combustion engine has a much higher power-to-weight ratio than a steam engine.

The first internal combustion engines were developed in the 1860s and 1870s. They used gas as a fuel. In the 1880s, two German engineers, Gottlieb Daimler and Karl Benz, built internal combustion engines that were similar to those used in cars today. They also built two of the first proper cars.

The car takes shape

In the USA and Europe, many engineers began making their own cars. Cars started to look less like carriages without the horses, and more like cars as we would recognize them today. There were technical developments, such as the addition of gears, clutches and drive shafts. By the end of the nineteenth century, the car was ready to take over the world.

Cars for all

Henry Ford

Henry Ford (1863–1947) was an American industrialist. He began work as a mechanic's apprentice and then became a mechanical engineer. He designed and built cars in his spare time before starting the Ford Motor Company in 1903.

The Model T assembly line in 1914. Radiators and wheels are lined up, ready to be added to each chassis.

The first cars that people were able to buy were built one-by-one by skilled coach-builders. They were large and luxurious, and only the very rich could afford them. To most people, they were just curiosities, not vehicles that they might ever buy for themselves. However, in the USA, a businessman called Henry Ford realized that if he built thousands of cars all the same, each one would be cheap to build – and cheap to buy. This was how the mass production of cars began.

The Model T

Henry Ford's Ford Motor Company began making its first car, called the Model T, in 1908. The Model T was a small, simple, cheap car. It was built on an assembly line from standard parts. In all, 15 million Model Ts were made and sold. In Europe, the Fiat and Austin companies began making small cars, too.

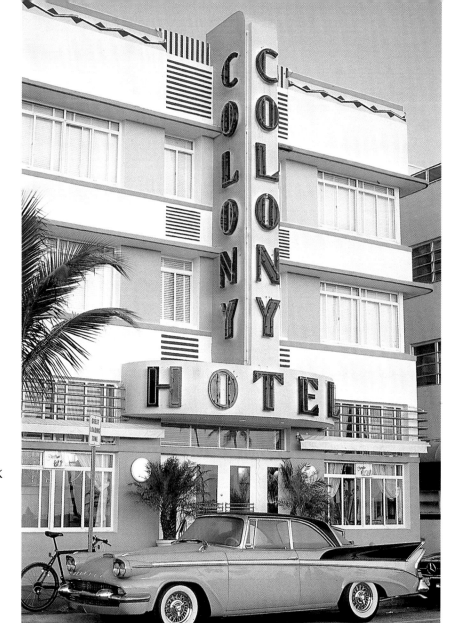

This 'gas guzzler' is a typical American car from the 1950s, when fuel efficiency was not important.

The spread of roads

As cars became cheaper, more and more people bought them and took to the roads. But most roads were designed to be used by the occasional horse and cart, not by dozens of cars. Existing roads had to be surfaced with smooth, long-lasting tarmac. New roads were designed with cars in mind.

As long-distance motoring became more popular, a new type of road, the motorway, was needed. It would allow cars to travel quickly between cities. The first motorways (called *autobahnen*) were built in Germany in the 1930s.

The drive for efficiency

In the 1950s and 1960s, people drove huge, inefficient, 'gas guzzling' cars, especially in the USA. But in the 1970s, the price of fuel rose greatly, and people also began to be concerned about the environmental effects of cars. Today, manufacturers try to make cars that use fuel as efficiently as possible. A car with low fuel consumption costs less money to run and so is likely to sell better than one that uses a lot of fuel.

HOW CARS WORK

Even on a short car journey, you will see dozens of different makes, shapes and sizes of car on the road. They might all look different, but underneath they are all very similar.

A car can be divided up into several parts, called components. Each component does a particular job. The main components are the body, the wheels, the engine and the transmission (which transfers the power from the engine to the wheels).

Car bodies

Most modern cars have a solid metal body. The body forms a cage to which all the other parts are attached. Folds in the metal make the body stiff, and the outside of the body forms the car's smooth outer surface. The doors and bonnet are made separately. Originally, cars were made up of a strong chassis with the body built on top. All the car's working parts were attached to the chassis.

A car body takes shape on a production line. There are small holes all over it, where other parts will be attached later.

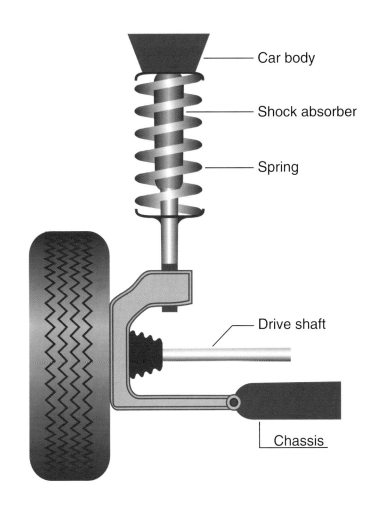

Car body

Shock absorber

Spring

Drive shaft

Chassis

A smooth ride

If a car's wheels were attached directly to its body, the passengers would feel every bump in the road, and the car body would eventually be damaged. Suspension stops this happening. Springs between the body and the wheels allow the wheels to move up and down over the bumps, giving a much smoother ride. Shock absorbers stop the body continuing to bounce up and down after a bump. Tyres on the wheels grip the road to stop the car skidding on corners and in the wet. They also help to absorb the impact of small bumps in the road.

Above **Each wheel has its own spring and shock absorber, which allow it to move up and down.**

Inside the body

Various fixtures and fittings inside the body make the car comfortable and safe to travel in. These parts include the seats and seat belts, the dashboard, air ducts and the radio.

Running through the body are bundles of electrical wires. The lights, the driver's instruments, heaters, window winders and numerous other parts are powered by electricity. When the engine is running, it turns a generator that makes electricity for the car. A battery provides electricity when the engine is stopped.

Right **The switches, dials and instruments on the dashboard are arranged so that the driver can see them easily and use them safely while on the move.**

Car engines

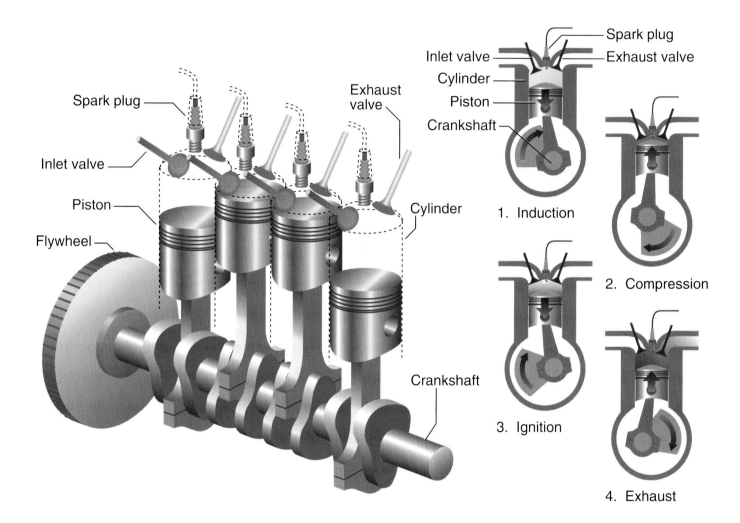

Spark plug

Inlet valve

Piston

Flywheel

Exhaust valve

Cylinder

Crankshaft

Spark plug
Inlet valve
Exhaust valve
Cylinder
Piston
Crankshaft

1. Induction

2. Compression

3. Ignition

4. Exhaust

A petrol engine works on a four-stroke cycle. The piston moves down, sucking a fuel-and-air mixture into the cylinders (induction). As it moves up, the fuel and air are squeezed into a small space (compression). A spark from a spark plug ignites the mixture (ignition), and the explosion pushes the piston down. It then moves up again, forcing out the exhaust gases.

Most cars have an internal combustion engine with four cylinders and pistons. The engine is turned when fuel explodes in the cylinders, pushing the pistons down. The moving pistons turn the crankshaft, which goes out of the engine to turn the wheels.

Fuel and exhaust

An engine needs a constant supply of fuel to keep it going. The fuel is stored in a fuel tank. From there, it is pumped along a pipe to a device called the carburettor. Here, it is made into a fine mist and mixed with air. This fuel-and-air mixture is sucked into the cylinders.

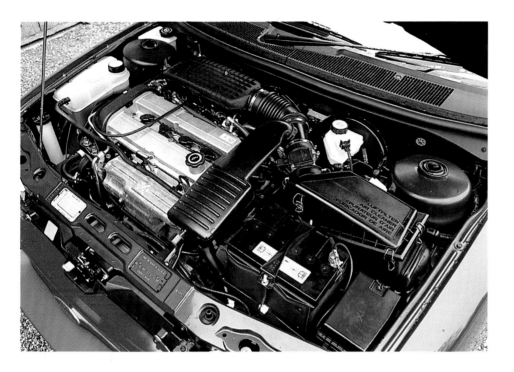

Under the bonnet of a family car. You can see the engine (top left) and the battery (bottom right).

In a petrol engine, like the one in the diagram on page 12, the fuel and air explode when the fuel is ignited by a spark from a spark plug. The other common type of engine is the diesel engine, which has no spark plugs. Instead, the fuel-and-air mixture is squeezed so much by the piston that it gets very hot and explodes by itself.

Once the fuel has burnt, waste gases are left in the cylinder. They pass into the exhaust system, which lets the gases escape gradually into the air. The exhaust is fitted with a silencer, so that you cannot hear the bangs as the fuel mixture explodes in the engine. Most exhausts also have a catalytic converter that stops some of the polluting gases getting into the air.

Cooling and lubricating

All the explosions and movements inside an engine make a lot of heat. To stop the engine overheating, cool water is pumped around it. The water gets hot, and so carries the heat away from the engine. The hot water flows through a radiator, where the heat escapes into the air. The cooled water then returns to the engine again.

The engine parts are kept lubricated by engine oil. Without oil, the metal parts would rub against each other. Friction would soon make them so hot that the metal would melt.

Turbochargers

Some sporty cars have a device called a turbocharger which gives the engine more power. It is a pump that forces air into the engine. The pump is made to turn by the fast-moving exhaust gases.

13

Starting, stopping and steering

A car has three controls that can be used to make it go faster or slower. The first is the accelerator, which controls the amount of power the engine produces. When the driver presses the accelerator pedal, more fuel is sprayed into the air that goes into the cylinders, making the strength of the explosions greater. The other controls are the gears and the brakes.

The gearbox

The engine is connected to the wheels via the gearbox. The engine works best when each cylinder fires several thousand times a minute. Using different gears means that the engine can work at this speed no matter how fast the wheels are turning. Low gears are for starting off. High gears are for driving at high speed.

In cars with a manual gearbox, the driver changes gear with a gear lever, pressing the clutch pedal at the same time. The clutch disconnects the engine from the gearbox while the change of gear is being made. An automatic gearbox changes gear automatically as the car speeds up and slows down.

This picture shows how complicated an automatic gearbox is inside. This gearbox has five different gears.

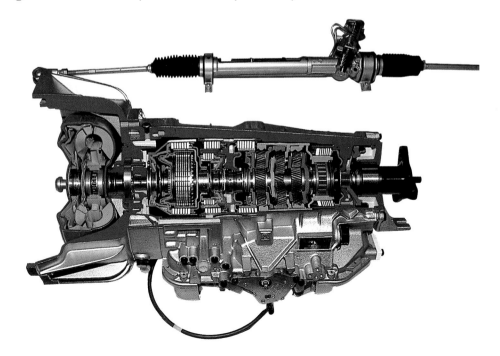

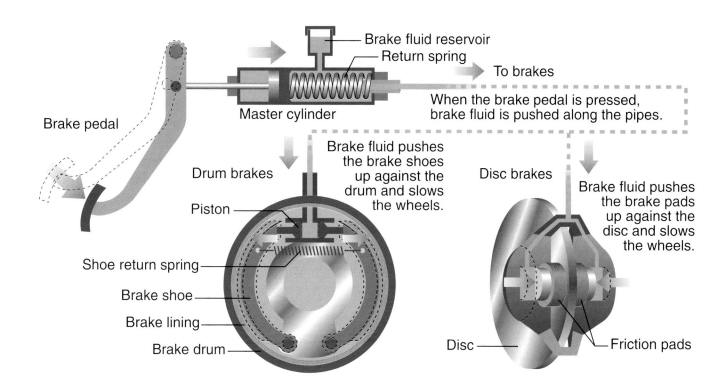

Brake fluid reservoir
Return spring
To brakes
When the brake pedal is pressed,
brake fluid is pushed along the pipes.
Master cylinder
Brake pedal
Drum brakes
Brake fluid pushes
the brake shoes
up against the
drum and slows
the wheels.
Piston
Disc brakes
Brake fluid pushes
the brake pads
up against the
disc and slows
the wheels.
Shoe return spring
Brake shoe
Brake lining
Brake drum
Disc
Friction pads

Brakes

Brakes are for slowing down and stopping the car. They come on when the driver presses the brake pedal. Most cars have two sets of brakes – brake pads on the front wheels and brake shoes on the rear wheels. The brakes are assisted by the engine, so the driver only has to press lightly on the brake pedal to slow the car.

Left and right

Turning the steering wheel makes a car turn to the left or right. When the driver turns the steering wheel, it moves a rod called the steering rack, which in turn makes the wheels swivel. Large and medium-sized cars have power steering, in which power from the engine helps to swivel the wheels. On most cars, it is only the front wheels that steer. A few cars have four-wheel steering, so all four wheels swivel at the same time. The rear wheels swivel in the opposite direction to the front wheels.

The braking system is full of special brake fluid. It transfers the pressure from a push on the brake pedal to the brake shoes and brake pads on the wheels.

CARS ON THE ROAD

There are hundreds of different designs of car for driving on ordinary roads. Of course, each manufacturing company wants its cars to look different from the cars made by its rivals. But differences in size and shape are there mainly because the cars are designed for different jobs. Normally, small cars are designed for short trips around towns, and larger cars are designed for long-distance travel.

Cars in town

In towns and cities, cars carry people to work and school, and to the shops and other amenities. They are also used to deliver goods to shops and homes. The streets are often full of cars, especially in the morning and evening rush hours. Small cars are designed for doing short journeys, especially around towns, that require a lot of starting, stopping and creeping along. This kind of driving uses up more fuel than long-distance driving, so town cars tend to have small, efficient engines, with a capacity of about 1000 cc. Small cars are also easier to manoeuvre into parking spaces.

Below **The Ford Ka is a typical modern, small, efficient, friendly-looking town car.**

Right **Up to six adults can fit into this 'people-mover'. It is useful for carrying people around town, and is also perfect for days out and holidays.**

Long distance by car

Larger cars are normally designed for long-distance travel – for days out, holiday journeys and business travel. Comfort and quietness are more important than they are in town cars. Engines are larger because more power is needed to get a heavier car moving, and to cruise efficiently at high speed. These cars also have more luggage space, more comfortable seats, air-conditioning and sophisticated entertainment systems.

As a car moves along the road, it disturbs the air around it. The more it disturbs the air, the more the air tries to slow it down. The car has to use more power – and so more fuel – to keep moving quickly. Cars designed to travel at high speeds for long distances have a streamlined shape to help them move smoothly through the air.

Above **This US station wagon is more suitable for longer journeys than a 'town car'. It has a more powerful engine.**

Below **Traffic on one New York street is stopped by the red traffic light, to allow traffic on the other street to cross the junction.**

Slow and fast lanes

Busy city and town centres need traffic controls to keep the thousands of cars moving smoothly. Traffic lights allow cars travelling in different directions to cross junctions in turn. One-way systems reduce the number of junctions that are needed. Parking restrictions and car parks help to keep the streets free of parked cars.

In many countries, networks of motorways and bypasses make long-distance travel fast. The roads are designed with shallow gradients and sweeping bends, so drivers can keep to a steady speed instead of having to slow down repeatedly. There are few junctions, and two or three parallel lanes make overtaking easy. Service areas provide convenient places for refuelling.

Safety and comfort

Unfortunately, because there are millions of cars on the road, accidents do happen. Thousands of car passengers and pedestrians are killed and injured every year. All cars have special features that greatly reduce the risk of accidents happening. They are also designed to reduce the risk of injuries if an accident does occur.

Tyres and brakes

Skidding is a major cause of accidents. A car skids when its wheels stop turning and the tyres slide along the road. Once a car is in a skid, the brakes and steering are almost useless.

Deep water on the road can cause skidding, because the tyres can slide over the water's surface. The tread on the tyres helps to prevent this 'aquaplaning' by pushing water away to the sides. Skidding also happens when the driver applies the brakes too quickly. The wheels 'lock' and the tyres slide. Many larger cars have an anti-lock braking system (ABS) to prevent this happening. Electronic circuits detect that the wheels are about to lock and automatically release the brakes slightly.

The tread pattern of a tyre. As the tyre rolls along a wet road, water is squeezed along the grooves so that the tyre can grip the road.

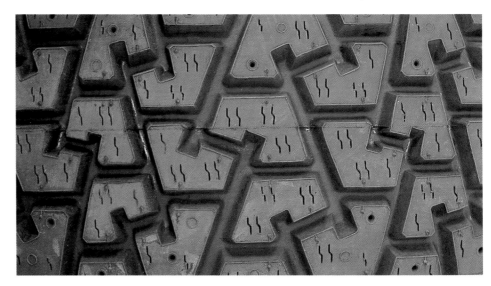

Seat belts and air bags

Many injuries are caused when passengers are thrown about inside their car, or through the windscreen, during a collision. Seat belts hold passengers in their seats. Some cars are fitted with air bags, which inflate almost instantly in a collision to prevent the driver and front-seat passenger from hitting the steering wheel and dashboard. Head restraints help prevent 'whiplash' injuries, which are caused by people's heads being thrown backwards if their car is hit from behind.

Side-impact bars and crush zones

Car bodies are designed to collapse in some places but not others. They have 'crush' zones at the front and back that collapse slowly and absorb some of the energy of the crash. Side-impact bars inside the doors help to protect the passengers if the car is hit from the side.

Accident testing

All new models of car are put through simulated accidents (above) to test how safe they are. The tests are recorded by high-speed cameras. Dummies inside the car record the types of injury the passengers might suffer.

Left **In an accident, this car's crush zones crumple up, but the passenger compartment stays in shape.**

SPECIAL CARS

The cars that most people own are made in their hundreds of thousands, or even millions. Because they are produced in such large numbers, they are called production cars. However, some cars are one-off cars, or are built in limited numbers or for special jobs. Some of these are based on production cars, with extra parts added, but others are completely different.

Emergency vehicles

Cars used by the police and other emergency services are often created from production cars. For example, standard police patrol cars are based on family saloon cars. The companies that make them buy them as standard cars from the manufacturer and customize them. They add emergency lights and two-way radios, and paint them in police colours. Emergency vehicles, especially police traffic patrol cars, often have more powerful engines than normal cars.

This production car has been adapted for use by the Danish police force.

This wacky custom car was originally a Morris Minor.

Custom cars

Some car enthusiasts build their own custom cars. They start with a normal production car (usually an old one), take it apart and rebuild it to their own design. They change the shape of the body and sometimes add a new, more powerful engine. They normally finish the car off by decorating it with a fabulous painted design and polishing the metalwork until it shines.

Vans

Vans used by tradespeople are often based on family cars. Only the body is different. Some of the windows are replaced with metal panels so that expensive tools and equipment can be hidden away inside.

Luxury cars

For many people, cars are not just a vehicle for getting them from one place to another. Their car is a symbol of their importance in society or business. For very important or very rich people, a luxury car is almost essential. They might even have a chauffeur to drive it for them.

Top of the range

Many car manufacturers build luxury versions of their large cars. These 'top-of-the-range' cars are often driven by wealthy business people. The difference between a top-of-the-range car and a standard car is mainly in the materials used in its interior. The seats are covered in leather, the carpets are deep and luxurious, and polished wood replaces plastic.

Rolls-Royce

Some car manufacturers produce only luxury cars. Each one takes far more time to build than a normal car, and far fewer are sold. Of course, they are also much more expensive to buy. The most famous name in luxury cars is Rolls-Royce.

A Rolls-Royce Silver Shadow, built in 1977. On top of the radiator is the famous Rolls-Royce emblem – a silver statue of a winged woman.

A stretched limousine in the USA.
The structure of a car like this has
to be especially strong to stop the
long body sagging.

Limousines

A limousine is a large, luxurious car, driven by a chauffeur.
Inside a limousine, the front seats, where the chauffeur sits, are
separated from the rear seats by a glass screen. This gives the
passengers privacy. In the back of the car, there is space for the
passengers to work and relax. Larger versions have luxury
features, such as drinks cabinets and televisions. A stretched
limousine is one that has been made longer by adding more
bodywork between the wheels. The longer your stretched
limousine, the more important you are.

Coachwork

The first luxury cars were built in two parts. The chassis, engine
and other mechanical parts were built and assembled by the
car manufacturer. Then it was passed to a coach-builder, who
added the bodywork and interior fittings. When you bought a
car, you could specify which coach-builder you wanted to
work on it.

Off the road

Most cars are designed to travel on smooth, tarmac-covered roads. Off-road vehicles are designed to travel over rough ground – unsurfaced roads, rutted dirt tracks and even across country, where there is no road at all. Off-road vehicles are useful on farms, and for driving in areas of the world where there are few tarmac roads. They are also useful for the armed forces and rescue services. Special features are needed for off-road driving.

Four-wheel drive

In most ordinary cars, the engine powers just two of the wheels, but in off-road vehicles, the engine drives all four wheels. This is called four-wheel drive, or 'four-by-four'. Four-wheel drive gives the vehicle lots of extra grip on slippery surfaces and steep hills.

Four-wheel drive and chunky tyres mean this small truck can be driven over ground where ordinary cars would get stuck.

Tracks

For especially difficult terrain, some off-road vehicles have their rear wheels (or even all their wheels) replaced by tracks. Tracks spread a vehicle's load over a much bigger area than even the biggest tyres, and give a huge amount of grip. The tracks are driven round by a toothed wheel, which pulls the track backwards, making the vehicle roll across the top of the track.

Left The tracks on armoured personnel carriers allow them to be used to reach remote areas in bad weather.

Engines and gears

Off-road vehicles must be able to climb very steep hills, and they often have to pull heavy trailers. These vehicles have large engines, three or four times as powerful as the engine in a normal family car. They have extra 'low' gears, too, to help them climb hills. Four-wheel-drive vehicles often have two gear settings – one provides lots of low gears for off-road travel and the other gives higher gears for normal driving.

Wheels and tyres

For extra grip in muddy conditions, off-road vehicles need large, chunky tyres with deep treads. Large tyres help to spread the vehicle's load over the soft ground, making it less likely to sink in. Large wheels also make the space between the ground and the bottom of the body (which is called the clearance) larger. This helps to prevent the bottom of the vehicle scraping or getting stuck on bumpy ground.

MOTOR SPORT

Formula 1

The Formula 1 World Championship takes place every year. There are sixteen Grand Prix races in the series, and most of them are held in Europe. Each race lasts for about two hours. Points are awarded to the first six cars in each race. There are in fact two championships: one for the driver who wins most points, and one for the car constructor whose cars win most points.

Motor racing is an entertaining hobby for some people and an international sport for others. Many different events make up motor sport. Every weekend, there are small local rallies and races, such as kart racing, where there might be more drivers than spectators. On the other hand, races of the FIA Formula 1 World Championship are watched on television by millions of people around the world. Some major car manufacturers run their own motor-racing teams. Taking part in motor sport gives them an important opportunity to advertise their products.

Motor-racing history

The first proper motor race was held in France in 1894, on public roads from Paris to Rouen. Gradually, the two main types of racing that we have today – racing at speed around a track and rallying – emerged. Some races, such as the Le Mans 24-hour race in France and the Indianapolis 500 in the USA, have become classic events. Modern materials and technology mean that motor racing is far safer today than it was a few decades ago.

A huge crowd watches the cars parade around the oval track before the start of the Indianapolis 500 race.

Track racing

Most motor races take place on purpose-built motor-racing tracks. A race normally consists of several laps of the track. Some tracks have several bends, both sharp and sweeping, while others are smooth, oval shapes with banked curves. Purpose-built racing cars, saloon cars and karts all race on tracks.

Rallying

A rally is a race over public roads and rough tracks. It is a gruelling test of a car's reliability and the skill of its driver. Some rallies last just one day, but others last for several days, and a large back-up team is then needed for each car. There are different classes, such as those for cars with four-wheel drive and those for cars with two-wheel drive. There are also amateur and professional drivers, but they can all take part in the same race.

A rally car hurtles through a muddy puddle during the four-day RAC rally, held each year in Britain.

Stock cars

Stock cars are old production cars that are no longer fit to drive on the roads. Safety features are added to them before they are used in stock-car racing and driven to destruction on the track.

Sports production cars

Some types of racing car are specialized versions of the production cars that you can buy to drive on the road. On the other hand, a few production cars are road-going versions of cars that were originally designed to be driven only on the race track. There are also many production cars that are designed to look like racing cars. They have better performance than ordinary cars, but nothing like the performance of proper racing cars.

Changes for racing

For racing, a car must be able to accelerate quickly, travel fast and slow down quickly for corners. Good acceleration and good top speed mean having a powerful engine (often with a turbocharger) and a lightweight, streamlined car. Powerful brakes, wide, smooth, track-gripping tyres and strengthened suspension are also needed. After all these changes, there is really only the body left from the original car. Inside the body, strong roll bars stop the roof caving in if the car rolls over in an accident.

Saloon-car racing on a race track. These racing cars are based on standard family cars.

Above **One car that uses many of the features found on Formula 1 racing cars is the Maclaren F1. Unfortunately, it costs twice as much as a Rolls-Royce!**

Racers on the road

You cannot just take a racing car and drive it on public roads. It would probably be illegal, because the car would not have some of the features required by law, such as mudguards and headlights. However, some people convert racing cars so that they can use them on the road.

The features developed by racing-car constructors to make their cars faster than their rivals' are sometimes used on top-of-the-range production cars. Sometimes, they eventually become standard features on every car. An example of this is 'active' suspension, which detects small bumps in the road and adjusts the suspension to iron out the bumps.

Racing cars are not usually allowed to be driven on the roads, but during the Monaco Grand Prix, the Formula 1 drivers have the roads of Monte Carlo all to themselves.

Built for racing

This Formula 1 car keeps its grip on the track with wide tyres. The 'wings' at the front and back press the tyres more firmly on to the road as air flows over them.

Purpose-built racing cars have similar components to normal cars, but the components are specially designed to give the car the best performance possible. Most racing cars are built to race at certain standards, such as Formula 1. To make the race fair, all the cars that race against each other must be about the same size and have the same-sized engines.

Racing engines

A racing-car engine must produce as much power as possible for its weight (in other words, it needs a high power-to-weight ratio). Most ordinary cars have a four-cylinder engine. Racing-car engines can have ten or even twelve cylinders, and they turn at a much higher speed. This makes them complicated, but they can be four or five times more powerful. They are made of aluminium, a light metal, to reduce the weight.

A huge Bentley racing car on the banked racing track at Brooklands in Britain, in 1929.

Old racers

The fastest modern racing cars are small and light. In the very early days of motor racing, the fastest cars were the ones with the biggest engines. They were enormous – three or four times as big as a modern engine, which meant the cars had to be enormous, too.

The land speed record

The most famous record in motor sport is for the fastest car. It is known as the world land speed record. It currently stands at 1019.5 kph (633.5 mph), and was set in 1983 by a British jet-powered car called Thrust 2.

Drag racing

A drag race is a race between two cars along a straight track about half a kilometre long. The first car to reach the end of the course wins. The cars have very high acceleration and huge rear wheels for plenty of grip.

Left **Drag-racing cars have parachutes to slow them down quickly at the end of their race.**

VEHICLES AT WORK

Cars are not the only vehicles on the road. The two other main types of vehicle are public transport vehicles, such as buses, and haulage vehicles, such as articulated lorries. There are also numerous specialized vehicles, from fire engines and road-cleaning trucks to electric milk floats.

Public transport

Public transport vehicles are vehicles on which people pay to travel. Public transport is especially important in towns and cities, where traffic congestion can be reduced by a lot of people travelling in one vehicle, such as a bus, instead of in separate vehicles. It is also useful for people who need to travel between towns and cities but do not have a car. For many people, especially in the poorer countries of the world, public transport is their only form of transport.

Highly-decorated truck-taxis are a common sight in some countries. This one in the Philippines has been adapted from a Jeep and is called a jeepney.

Above **Minibuses like these are designed for short journeys around towns.**

Buses in towns

Buses built for use around towns and cities have special features to make them easy and safe for passengers to use. Wide doors allow people to enter or leave two at a time, and some buses have separate doors for getting on and off. The steps are designed to make getting on and off easier for elderly people and people with young children. Inside, there are plenty of hand-holds to grab while the bus is moving. City buses do not need to travel at high speed, but they do need powerful engines for pulling away quickly from stops.

Buses use bus-only lanes in towns and cities so that they can move quickly through the traffic. In some cities, buses can lock on to special tracks next to the roads and then operate in a similar way to trams.

Long distance by bus

Buses used for long-distance transport (which are often called coaches) have different features to city buses. The passengers are likely to be on the bus much longer, so they need more comfortable seats. There is space for luggage in a hold under the seats, and there may be a toilet. Modern coaches sometimes have video screens for showing films during the journey, and refreshments are sometimes available.

Below **Greyhound buses carry people on long journeys between cities in the USA.**

Haulage vehicles

Haulage vehicles carry goods from place to place. Even on a short road journey, you will probably see haulage vehicles in many different shapes and sizes, from small vans making local deliveries to enormous long-distance trucks. Trucks have powerful diesel engines and perhaps a dozen gears to help them pull heavy loads uphill. The driver's cab is designed for comfort, and in bigger trucks it even has a bed for the driver.

Truck types

There are three main types of truck: rigid trucks, articulated trucks and drawbar trucks.

A rigid truck is in one piece. The cab and the body are fixed to a chassis.

An articulated truck (or 'artic') comes in two parts, called the tractor unit and the semi-trailer. These can be separated so that the tractor unit can haul different semi-trailers.

A drawbar truck is a combination of a rigid truck and a trailer. The two parts are linked by a rigid tow bar. The front axle of the trailer can turn to steer the trailer round corners.

Left **An articulated truck carrying logs in Australia. The pipe on top of the cab carries exhaust gases into the air.**

Truck bodies

You can think of trucks as having two parts. The first part is the chassis and cab. The second is the cargo-carrying body that fits on top of the chassis. Two trucks that carry different types of cargo can have exactly the same chassis and cab.

Road versus rail

It takes hundreds of trucks to carry as much cargo as one train, and trucks create far more congestion and pollution. But road transport is more convenient than rail, because trucks can deliver their cargoes to almost anywhere, whereas trains can only go where there are railway lines. Some countries, especially mountainous ones, do not have railway networks, so trucks are the only practical way of transporting goods.

This tractor unit is pulling a trailer with fabric sides, called curtain sides. It carries general cargo.

Special vehicles

There are all sorts of vehicles that carry out just one particular job. They might not be designed to be driven on the road, so you might never see them. Many consist of machines mounted on truck bodies, such as fire engines and breakdown trucks. If you visit an airport, look out for the dozens of specialized vehicles used there, such as aircraft tractors, refuelling trucks, baggage trains and catering trucks.

An aircraft-towing tractor manoeuvring an aircraft. Its low body keeps it away from the aircraft's nose.

Construction vehicles

Many specialized vehicles can be found at work on construction sites. Diggers, earth movers, dumper-trucks and mobile cranes are all designed for working off the road on rough, muddy ground. They also have moving parts (such as a digger's arms) that are worked by hydraulic rams.

Electric vehicles

Electric vehicles are powered by an electric motor, which runs off batteries carried inside the vehicle. When the batteries run down, they can be recharged. Electric power is good for slow, stop-start journeys. Some delivery vans, such as milk floats, are electric vehicles. So are golf buggies. You can find out about electric cars on page 41.

Vehicles on the Moon

There are a handful of vehicles on the Moon. The Apollo 15 spacecraft carried the first two-person buggy, the Lunar Roving Vehicle, which ran on electric power. In order to be carried in the spacecraft, it had to be very light. It also had to fold away inside the smaller lunar module that actually landed on the Moon. Astronauts used it to explore the Moon's surface and collect rock samples. Another vehicle on the Moon is the remote-controlled probe Lunokhod, which landed in 1970. It explored for several months, controlled by operators on Earth.

The Lunar Roving Vehicle driving across the rocky surface of the Moon.

THE FUTURE

Cars and taxis jamming Park Avenue in New York City, USA. As traffic jams in cities worsen, the car is no longer a quick and convenient method of transport.

You have seen how cars were invented and how cars and roads have developed during the twentieth century. What is likely to happen in the twenty-first century?

No doubt cars will look different and be easier to drive – they might even drive themselves. They will also become safer. But driving might become impossible unless some of the environmental problems created by cars are solved. Experts estimate that the number of cars on the world's roads will double in twenty years. This will create 'gridlock' in many cities. Unless exhaust emissions become cleaner, it will also mean more air pollution.

Cars and the environment

Cars create problems for the environment in two ways – the roads they travel on spoil the landscape, and their exhaust gases contain polluting chemicals. Some of these chemicals are poisonous, and some contribute to global warming. One way to help solve these problems would be to reduce the number of cars. This would mean persuading people to use public transport instead. Governments could increase the taxes on car fuel and use the money to improve public transport, but policies such as this would be unpopular with most drivers.

The problems caused by pollution, especially in cities, were first seen in the 1970s, as the number of cars grew rapidly. Since then, there have been many improvements, such as lead-free petrol and catalytic converters. In some countries, cars must have an 'emissions test' every year, to make sure they are not producing too many harmful gases. The number of cars going into city centres has been restricted in some areas. One answer to city-centre pollution is the electric car (see page 41). Another would be to discourage people from bringing their cars into city centres by making them pay a toll. Systems are being developed that could recognize each car as it passes a toll point and could then send the driver a bill in the post.

New roads

As the number of cars increases, congestion gets worse. New roads have to be built and existing roads widened to keep the traffic flowing smoothly. These new roads soon seem to fill up with new cars, so more roads are needed, and so the problem goes on. Some people argue that building more and more roads is destroying the environment, without solving the problem of congestion.

There are often protests on the sites of new roads. Here, security guards are pulling a road protester away from a construction site. There are many more protesters in the background.

Cars of the future

Almost from the time the car industry began, designers have been showing what they think the car of the future will look like. These 'concept' cars usually look very different from the cars we are used to seeing on the roads. In reality, the appearance of cars changes quite slowly, and, underneath, cars still have the same basic components. However, advances in technology mean that cars are becoming cleaner, more fuel-efficient, and safer and easier to drive.

New forms of power

Two of the most important features of a modern car are fuel efficiency and low exhaust emissions. Both of these depend on the type of engine in the car, and how efficiently it works. Most cars will continue to be powered by internal combustion engines, but they will also become cleaner and more efficient.

A battery-powered Citroen AX being recharged at a garage in France. It was being used in a project to find out whether electric cars could be used successfully for town driving.

The obvious alternative to the internal combustion engine is the electric motor. The problem with electric cars is that the batteries can only provide enough power to travel about 100 km, and they have to be recharged regularly. However, electric cars are well suited to towns and cities, where most journeys are short, and the cars can be recharged at night. Only the invention of a very long-lasting but powerful battery will make electric cars suitable for general motoring.

An alternative to the electric car is the hybrid car, which has electric motors and an internal combustion engine to keep the batteries charged. In areas of the world where long hours of sunshine are guaranteed, electric cars could have solar panels to turn sunlight into electricity for the motors.

This car, the General Motors EV1, is the first electric-powered car to go into full production.

Car security

Car theft is a major problem in many countries. Manufacturers have tried to tackle the problem by fitting more and more sophisticated locks. In a remote-control central locking system, for example, each car has a unique security code that is transmitted from the key to the car. Unfortunately, thieves can record the number and make their own keys. Manufacturers have responded by developing keys that randomly change the security code each time.

Smart cars

It is likely that the cars of the future will be smart cars. 'Smart' machines are ones that appear to be intelligent because they are controlled by a computer. Smart cars will have on-board computers to control almost every function – the engine efficiency, the brakes, the air bags, and so on. Even now, a few top-of-the-range cars have as much computer power as the Apollo 11 spacecraft which landed on the Moon in the 1960s. One of the latest supercars, the Maclaren F1, has a computer that records every detail of the car's performance and sends the information down the telephone to the manufacturer.

Easy driving

In countries where there are many long, straight roads, cars have had cruise controls, which keep the car going at a constant speed, for many years. In the future, cars might be able to keep a certain distance from the car in front automatically. Because a computer can react very much faster than a human, this distance could be much smaller than would normally be safe.

This is what a motorway of the future might look like. Keeping vehicles in convoy like this would allow more of them to use the roads at any one time.

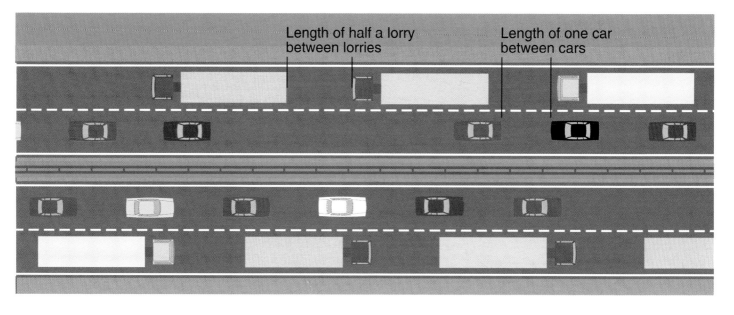

Length of half a lorry between lorries

Length of one car between cars

In the centre of this dashboard is a computerized automatic navigation map. It shows the driver exactly where he or she is and gives directions to the destination.

The impossible-to-crash car

Many cars already have an anti-lock braking system, which helps to prevent skidding. Cars of the future are likely to have more safety devices like this. Ideas that are already being tested include: video cameras that detect if the driver is falling asleep or is too close to the car in front; a system that automatically reduces speed if the car is being driven too fast around a corner; and multiple air bags that inflate just in the area where the passengers are likely to need them in an accident.

In-car navigation systems

You can already buy in-car electronic maps that tell you the quickest way to your destination and provide information about hotels, garages and other facilities. The latest systems are linked to the satellite global positioning system (GPS), which tells the car exactly where it is on the map. Other systems warn of congestion ahead and plan alternative routes. In the future, all cars are likely to have this sort of navigation system.

DATE CHART

1769 French soldier Nicholas Cugnot builds a steam tractor, designed for pulling cannon.

1803 A steam-powered coach makes a 16-km journey through London, reaching speeds of 14 kph.

1883 German engineer Gottlieb Daimler builds the first successful petrol engine.

1885 German engineer Karl Benz builds the first successful petrol-driven car, a three-wheeler.

1886 Gottlieb Daimler builds the first four-wheeled car.

1891 The first electrically-powered car is built in the USA. It could not go nearly as far or as fast as cars with petrol engines.

1892 Rudolph Diesel invents a completely new type of engine – now known as the diesel engine.

1894 The first proper motor race is held in France. It starts in Paris and finishes in Rouen.

1901 The first car with a layout similar to today's cars, the Daimler Mercedes, is built.

1902 Drum brakes and disc brakes are introduced; air-conditioning is introduced in cars made in the USA.

1903 The first vehicle with tracks instead of wheels (a tractor) is demonstrated in Britain.

1906 Charles Rolls and Henry Royce form the Rolls-Royce company.

1908 Henry Ford sets up a factory to make cars by mass production. The car built there was the Model T Ford.

1910 The automatic gearbox is invented in Germany.

1914 In the USA, Dodge builds the first car to have a steel body-shell, instead of a chassis with the bodywork built on top.

1918 In New York, USA, the first three-colour traffic lights are installed for traffic control.

1923 One-and-a-half million Model T Fords are sold in this year alone.

1926 The first front-wheel-drive car is introduced in France. Before this, all cars had rear-wheel drive.

1930 s The first motorways are built in Germany and Italy.

1936 Production of the Volkswagen Beetle starts in Germany. More than twenty million Beetles have been made since.

1959 A classic small car, the Austin-Morris Mini, is launched in Britain.

1971 Apollo 15 lands on the Moon. It carries a Lunar Roving Vehicle in which astronauts drive about on the lunar surface.

1973 Oil-producing companies in the Middle East cut off supplies of fuel to Europe and the USA. The price of fuel soars.

1974 Catalytic converters are introduced on new cars built in the USA.

1975 Lead-free petrol goes on sale for the first time in the USA.

1983 The jet-powered car Thrust 2 sets the land speed record in Nevada, USA.

1985 Several companies around the world develop in-car navigation systems.

1987 A solar-powered car called Sunraycer drives across Australia using only energy from the sun.

1996 The first electric-powered production car, the General Motors EV1, goes into production.

GLOSSARY

acceleration Getting faster. Deceleration is getting slower.

accelerator A pedal that controls the amount of fuel that goes into the engine of a car.

anti-lock braking system (ABS) A braking system in a car that helps to stop the car skidding if it has to stop suddenly.

assembly line A place in a factory where the parts of a car or other machine are put together in sequence.

automatic gearbox A gearbox that changes the gears automatically as the car speeds up and slows down.

battery A store of electricity.

catalytic converter The part of a car's exhaust system that turns some of the harmful gases made by the engine into harmless gases.

chassis A strong framework on to which the parts of a truck are attached. Some old cars also have a chassis.

clutch A device that disconnects the engine from the gearbox. The driver presses the clutch pedal while changing gears.

coach-builder A craftsperson who built the bodies, seats and furnishings of coaches.

customize To change a product to meet a customer's specific requirements.

diesel engine A type of internal combustion engine used in some cars and most trucks and buses.

drive shaft A rod that links the gearbox to a wheel. It is controlled by the gearbox and turns the wheels.

engine capacity The total volume of all the cylinders in an internal combustion engine.

four-wheel drive A system in which a vehicle's engine turns all four of its wheels.

gearbox A box between the engine and the wheels that changes the speed at which the engine turns the wheels.

generator A device that makes electricity when it is turned. A car has a generator that is turned by the engine.

global positioning system (GPS) A very accurate navigation system. A GPS receiver picks up radio signals from satellites.

global warming The gradual heating-up of the air in the atmosphere. It is caused by the gas carbon dioxide trapping heat from the sun.

gradients Slopes. The term is usually used to describe the sloping sections of roads or railways.

gridlock A major traffic jam, in which all routes are blocked and traffic is unable to move at all.

hydraulic rams Pistons that are made to move by pressure produced by a liquid being forced through a pipe.

internal combustion engine An engine in which fuel burns inside the engine, making small explosions. Petrol and diesel engines are internal combustion engines.

karts Light vehicles with small engines.

lead-free petrol Petrol that has no lead in it. Standard petrol contains a small amount of lead to help make the engine run more smoothly, but lead is a poisonous substance.

mass production Manufacturing things, such as cars, in very large numbers. Identical parts are used in each item and assembled on a production line.

power-to-weight ratio The power that an engine produces compared to how heavy the engine is.

production car A car made in a factory by mass production.

solar panel An electronic device that turns the energy in sunlight into electrical energy.

suspension The part of a car or truck, between the body and the wheels, that absorbs the impact of bumps in the road, making the ride smoother.

transmission The part of a car that transfers power from the engine to the wheels. The clutch, gearbox and drive shaft are part of the transmission.

tread The outer part of a tyre, which is in contact with the road.

turbocharger A pump in some engines that pumps air into the cylinders. It increases the power of the engine.

two-wheel drive A system in which a vehicle's engine turns two of its wheels (either the two front wheels or the two rear wheels).

FIND OUT MORE

Books to read

Science Discovery: Transport by Brian Williams (Wayland, 1995)
Inventions in Science: The Car by Steve Parker (Watts Books, 1992)
The World's Transport: Road Travel by Tim Wood (Wayland, 1992)

There are many monthly car magazines, covering family cars, sports cars, new cars, old cars and all kinds of motor sport. There are also several truck and bus magazines. Look for them in your local newsagent.

Places to visit:

The National Motor Museum, Beaulieu, Hampshire.
A large collection of old and new cars.

The Science Museum, Exhibition Road, London.
Examples of cars (including a Benz of 1888 and steam-powered vehicles) and fire engines. It also has exhibits on engines, finding fuels and pollution.

The Leyland Truck Museum, Leyland, Lancashire.
A collection of historic trucks, including ones made by the Leyland company.

Transperience, Bradford, West Yorkshire.
A collection of buses and trams.

The Motor Show, National Exhibition Centre, Birmingham.
A huge exhibition of cars held in autumn each year, where new manufacturers show their latest models and their ideas for the future.

INDEX